Sista Chat

Sista's, Lets Chat

Cassandra Iphigenia Williams

authorHOUSE®

AuthorHouse™
1663 Liberty Drive
Bloomington, IN 47403
www.authorhouse.com
Phone: 1-800-839-8640

First published by AuthorHouse 06/9/2011

ISBN: 978-1-4634-1760-4 (sc)
ISBN: 978-1-4634-1761-1 (e)
ISBN: 978-1-4634-1762-8 (dj)

Library of Congress Control Number: 2011910036

Printed in the United States of America

Dedication

I have to dedicate this book to my Husband Paul! Not only for giving me the idea and encouragement to complete this project. But also for the love,encouragement and fun we have had through out our 27 year marriage.

Thank you Bobula!

Introduction

The word Sista in this book refers to the kin- ship of all my Sister's in the world. Not just for the Sista's of color. We as women have so much in common. Unfortunately we as women make many of the same mistakes that bring sorrow to our lives. Especially in the male/female relationship department!

This book is meant as a wake up call to all my Sista's. It's purpose is not only to shine a light on the most common mistakes but also for the light within you to began shinning so that it may be noticed by others. If you are in need of truthful in your face advice, open the pages of this book and take the journey

Table of Contents

If you are a confident women in a happy,productive,loving relationship, this book is not for you. What ever your doing,, keep on doing it girlfriend! If you and your Man are doing well, continue on. You don't need my advice and as a sidebar, take no advice from anyone who's relationships are always in turmoil. How can they give you any advice when they can't help themselves!

On the other hand, if your the one who keeps falling for Mr. Wrong, or can't seem to find a good Man or who's male/female relationships are always troubled, then the advice I give you sure as hell can't make things worse.

Who am I? And who do I think I am to be giving you advice? I think that I am very special. In fact I feel I have been given a gift! (I think everyone has special things about themselves to offer the world if they just take the time to discover them). All my life, I've been one of those persons others have come to in order to confide in. For a long time, I wasn't sure why. But in speaking to a Friend one day, He pointed out that is was something in my spirit they recognized. He stated " You seem to really listen and try to understand what it is others feel". I also believe that every hurt,regret disappointment and mistake we make in our lives also serve to teach us something we need to know. We can also take advantage of the mistakes that others have made and learn from them. You don't have to fall off the same bridge that your friend fell off of to know that when she hit the ground, it hurt!

I am the wife of one Man for 27 years now..The Mother of 3 handsome young Men and the Grandmother of the most beautiful boy in the world. I have a loving,caring Husband who lives with me in knowledge. In fact, it was my Husband who encouraged me to write this book. He often tells me that I should charge my girlfriends for all the advice I give them. He said I should open up a web site called www.askCassandra.com. I just may do that in the future. On more than one occasion I've been told by my girlfriends that "I wish I had what you and your Husband have together". After hearing that more than once,it caused me to stop and think. Just what is it that my Husband and I have and how can I use that knowledge to help others? How can I share that knowledge with others. Not my Husband of course, but what it is that we have or do that could be passed on to others. I believe that God has given me a type of wisdom. A gift, a type of talent for putting things in a way that relates to others situations. A type of common sense. We all have a type of common sense but some of us just don't use it. Some of the advice I give you may seem old fashion but you know what? Wisdom remains wisdom through out the ages just as truth remains truth. Times may change as well as clothing but as the Bible says " There is nothing new under the sun".

This book is called Sista Chat but is not meant exclusively for Women of color. But for Women of all ages, creeds and colors. It seems to me that women (no matter the color) make the same mistakes when it comes to Men and are in need of some enlightenment. Someone needs to shine a light on the most common mistakes we as women make. And if possible show a way around them. Well tighten your seat belt, because the journey starts now. For some of you, it will be a bumpy road. Here we go!

The Journey

The journey begins and ends with You! The destination is a better understanding of the knowledge and depths of yourself. You may ask, what does knowing myself have to do with how to get and keeping a Man? What is it about knowing me that helps me to have a happy, productive relationship? Those of you who did ask the question are the ones in real need of my assistance. As you know, through out time, Women have been the nurtures .Expected to give of themselves, to be unselfish.

Some of us have taken that role too far. We feel incomplete without being able to nurture something and rarely take the time to nurture ourselves. We tend to look for something outside ourselves, usually a Man in order to feel complete. This is a falsehood and needs to be buried here and now! No one can complete you, but You! Stop looking outside yourself for something that can only be found and come from inside you! The person you need to respect and care for before you can really care for another, is Yourself! Some of you should actually take a vacation from men for awhile.

Take a vacation from all the drama involved and all the time and energy you devote to catching a man's attention and put that time and energy into yourself.

Find out about yourself, about what you need, what your goals are in life?

Find out what is wonderful about yourself. Learn to love yourself! Including every lump, bump,wrinkle and flaw that makes you unique Conceit is not necessary but a healthy acceptance, respect and love for yourself is absolutely necessary. You have to like and love yourself in order to find success in a happy, loving relationship. If you don't like your own company, how can you expect that another will? If you don't like and love yourself, what kind of recommendation is that for anyone else to see you in any other light than the one you shine on yourself?

All of this is very important! Because unless you take the time to journey into yourself, you may keep making the same mistakes over and over again, as some of you are doing right now! It is time to stop pointing the finger at fate and take some responsibility for the results you have achieved in your life. If your life resembles a train wreck, you had a hand in making it that way. If your life is endless drama, the one common denominator is you! Some of you won't like what I've just said. You may be whining about how none of this is your fault. You may bitch about how I just don't realize how bad luck follows you like a cloud. That I have no idea how and why it is you keep attracting the wrong kind of man. That you can't help yourself. I say again, In all the drama, the ups and the downs of your life, the one constant, the one common denominator is still You! If you continue the way you have been, you will be dooming yourself to continue making the same mistakes over and over again and again!

To get an idea of how special you really are and how you are seen by our Creator, there are two books I would recommend. The Bible and The Secret. We are created in the image of the most high! We are part of the whole! If you are unaware of that fact, make yourself aware of it now. Our thoughts and our opinions of ourselves are so vital, that they influence not only how we see ourselves but how we are seen and treated by others! When you like and love yourself, you are better equip to love others and have others love and respect you.

If you are unable to see your own beauty, no one else can show it to you. If you don't value yourself, if you don't see yourself as deserving,you are dooming yourself to relationships with Men who won't treat you as deserving and won't value you as you should be!

Some of the questions that need to be answered on your journey to self discovery are: Are you looking deep or are you being superficial? Just what is important to you? Do you consider yourself incomplete without a Man in your life? Just what holes are you trying to fill in your life? And who and what are you trying to fill them with? What is it that you are looking for in a Man? And just what is it that you are bringing to the table. These and other questions must be asked,answered and dealt with before you are ready for another relationship. If you don't deal with these issues now you are at high risk to continue perpetuating the same mistakes over and over again! STOP! Save yourself! Take the time to do the work that is needed. Give yourself the time, the love, the respect that you have been trying to get from others. Fill the holes and gaps in your life. Treat yourself first with deserving, respect and love. Fill the gaps in your life, the holes others have left in you life with the knowledge that you are indeed more than enough!

That you are the most special person you know. You have to find the person,you were meant to be. This will mean stepping out of your comfort zone in order to become the person you are truly meant to be. Until you arrive at your destination and really believe in the new you, act it! Act as if! Act as if you are a person deserving respect and love and all the great things that life has to offer. Act as if you are the most whole, together person you know. Treat yourself well. Treat yourself the way you would treat someone you admired. Treat yourself the way you would want others to treat you. When you allow yourself to be disrespected as if you are unworthy, it will perpetuate. You truly are the one who teaches others how to treat you. As part of the whole, you must realize that you are a creation of beauty. God did not make any junk! Know that you are indeed the Kings kid, no matter what you have been told in the past or by whom! You are the most special person, you know! Give yourself what you have been looking to other to give you. Happiness,love and joy are your birth rite! You are the party going someplace to happen! You bring the sunshine with you where ever you go! You have much more power than you realize. Power over your life and circumstances. If there has been no one in your life to tell you how special and wonderful you are, then start telling yourself! If you don't know where to start, read the Bible and the Secret. Keep a diary of all the wonderful descriptions God uses to describe his creation All the things you want to be, state them as facts daily. Make a positive mantra to be stated several times daily. Remember, you are the one who teach others how to treat you. By treating yourself well, you teach others to do the same. When you think your deserving, others will also. Are you starting to see just how important your opinion of yourself is, and how you teach others to respond to it?

Guess what? Until you change to this more loving, deserving version of yourself, you will continue to attract Men in your life who don't respect or treat you well! Take yourself on a vacation from the drama for a while. Take some time before getting into another relationship with a Man and get into a life long love affair with the person that matters most in your life. You!

We are responsible for our own circumstances and how we have arrived at this juncture in our lives. We are responsible for our own happiness. Cinderella, don't wait for Prince Charming to come along to solve all your problems in your life. You are your own savior! And now it's time to save yourself! When you are under the misconception that you alone are not enough and are waiting for someone else to come along and validate you, you give all your power away. You run the risk of repeating the same unhealthy relationships over and over again. It is you who must know and see yourself as complete. You are more than enough Woman for any Man! Get to the point and place where you began to hear your own voice (that inner voice).

Get to know the most essential, important person in your life. Get to know you!

Some of you won't recognize yourselves after you have stripped yourselves of all the old baggage you've been carrying around with you. All the old hurts and pains that have been your constant companions. This baggage that you have been carrying from relationship to relationship, allowing the past to cause problems in your present and in your future. Let it all go! It only poisons your now! You may feel uncomfortable at first because you have been use to carrying the extra weight but don't pick it back up! You have to keep telling yourselves that you are not the person you use to be, that you react differently and act differently than you use too. You know that you are complete, that you are perfect,whole,powerful,strong, loving,harmonious and happy. Change can be scary but it also presents opportunity for new and exciting things to happen in your life. Embrace the new you. Learn to love yourselves, that way others will learn to love you also. Don't get hung up on set backs. Forgive yourselves and move on. Just keep moving forward to the person you know, you have always wanted to be. Know that now, the only one who can stop you from reaching your destination, is you!

Road Map

Some of you may have a good sense of direction but that has never been my strong suite. What I really want to say here is that in order to find what you are looking for in life, some of us need direction. One of my friends (who is presently searching for Mr. Right) asked me one day if I could help her in her search. I asked her, what she was looking for in a Man?

Her response was "I don't know "! How can I help her(and how can she help herself) if she has no idea of what and who she is trying to find. What is it that you are looking for in a Man?Don't be superficial! A tight butt and a pretty face may be a nice benefit but if that is all there is too him, you have nothing! You need to know what qualities you are looking for in order to find them. What qualities in a Man compliments you and your personality. Some of you go for a type of Man that will never work in your life but never take the time to consider why? By the way, trying to redeem the bad boy type, never, never works! Admittedly there may be something magnetic about this type of Man. You and your love will not change a Man who has no wish to change. And why should he? As long as there is a long line of Women willing to try their skills upon him. If this is the type of Man you have been attracted to in the past(News to self) this never works and is a major waste of your time! There is a quote by Maya Angelo which states " When someone tells you who they are, believe them ". When a Man tells you or shows you that he is not a one women man or that he is unavailable to you, believe him! I have a Friend and for some reason when a Brother tells her that he is not Husband material,she takes it as a personal challenge to change his mind. She puts fort energy, time and money to make them see that she is the one for them. It always ends up the same way. She is broken hearted. Out of a lot of effort and at times money,while he has moved on to the next conquest as he said he would. You and your time is valuable. You no longer waste it on those who don't deserve you! As the Bible states " Don't cast pearls before swine".

The swine doesn't appreciate the effort. Get the message from the Man telling you he is not Husband material or exclusively yours ! Move on! Cut your loses! Don't spend one more minute in his presence or company! Save yourselves! Move on!! Remember who you are now. You are now a different person and you do things differently. You now see yourselves as valuable. As one who deserves all that God has to offer. Waste no more time with the swine in your life. Move on!

Make a List

Make a list of all the qualities and attributes you need and want in a Man. And don't be superficial! You need something deeper than a pretty face and tight ass. If all that comes with a deeper package, go for it. But look deep into yourselves and into the Man. What is it you really need and want in a relationship? A Man that respects and values you as a person. A Man that can make you laugh, who can make you feel special, adored and loved! A Man who cares as much about the Women in his life as he does himself. A Man is willing to be a Man in the relationship and one that not only can spell job, but one that can keep one! A lot of us settle for so much less. Some of us sadly have never been provided with the proper example of a Man in our lives. Our Father's bare the responsibility of showing us how a Man is to treat the Women in his life by being the example. By treating our Mothers well with reverence and respect. He also is to provide for his family, not only financially but also as a guide to life. By treating his Wife and Daughter with loving care, he also shows us what we are to expect from other men in our lives. Unfortunately some of us don't have positive Male role models or Father figures in our lives. And others of you have had a parade of Men, of so called Father figures in and out of your lives because of poor decisions made by your Mothers. Because of the poor example that you have been shown, you tend to follow the negative patterns because that is all you know. This is the reason it is important to fill in all the holes you have in your life. To come to the knowledge that you have the power to fill them in yourselves. Holes have a tendency to need to be filled. If you don't fill them with something positive, those gaps can be an avenue for negative to come into your life. Fill yours with self love,self deserving! Knowing that God has made you perfect, whole,strong and powerful. Knowing that he has left you the gift of love and joy. If you can find examples of happily married couples, observe their interactions. Remember we can learn from others experiences. Know this, no matter the example you have been shown in you life or by whom, you deserve to be treated with dignity,consideration, respect and love. Remember now that it is you, who teach others how to treat you. Start by treating yourselves well as you deserve to be treated. Reevaluate your idea of the perfect Man. Remember who you are now and that you don't repeat negative patterns as the old you did in the past. You don't allow anyone to treat you badly then go back for more of the same! You deserve a Man with intelligence, compassion,understanding,patience,empathy and loyalty! A Man willing to make changes if needed and is truly interested in your happiness as well as his own. A good relationship takes work but it is never one sided with one person doing all the work. If that is what is happening with you, then it really isn't a relationship. It's a job! Get a reality check! Pastor one said " A Man married a pair of legs and then found out that there was nothing above them ". Look for true values. Go for the true beauty in a Man. Integrity,responsibility, devotion to family, loyalty! Someone that builds you up and doesn't tare you down. Someone that sees you as the precious gift of God you truly are; There is also another saying " Beauty fades as the flower withers and you are left with the truth of what was always there".

Another thing that Women do that chaps my hide. I have seen some of you continue in unproductive,unhappy even abusive situations in relationships simply because of the time you have already invested in the Man. Reality check!! If time in the relationship was the key, your relationship would already be at the place you pretend that it is going but know that it is not! One more day in hell won't make any difference. One more day in that situation is one day too damn long. Get the hell out! Stop wasting your time going absolutely no where! Send that time that you are presently wasting on him, on yourselves! Until you convince yourselves that you deserve better! Ladies, I know it doesn't sound romantic to make as list. So what! It serves as as guide to keep us on task. Look for the life partner you deserve and don't settle for less And don't be afraid to be alone. Alone does not mean lonely! Use this time to spend with yourselves,learning to treat yourselves well. As a time to reflect and enjoy your own company. Take this time to make the list!!

Three Strikes Rule or Red Flag Rule

I like to refer to the dating process as a time of auditioning. Trying out the person you may spend the rest of your life with. By the way just mentioning a fact. The type of person you date is usually the type you end up marring. So a word to the wise! Don't date what you don't want to end up with. The definition of a strike or red flag is a serious deviation from your list of a defect in the person you are auditioning. One strike can be tolerated and two if there are extenuating circumstances. But never, never three! When you start over looking more than three strikes or excuses as to why you would continue on in a relationship that won't be positive for you,your acting as the old you. Stop and give serious thought as to why you would want to repeat mistakes you've already made. Why would you not deserve the attributes of the dream man on your list? Remember who you are now and that you deserve Mr. Right and not Mr. Right Now. Three strikes or red flags mean that he is out of there! Kicked to the curb! No refunds, no replays! Just out! Do not keep going over the same territory! Move on. He has failed his audition and it's time to go on the the next lucky candidate.

There are times when one strike is the deal breaker and no more time or effort will be devoted. There will be no second chances. In the case of physical,verbal or psychological abuse!, This will not be tolerated at all!! If you allow yourselves to be abused a first time, there will always,always be a second. No matter how sweetly he begs or how much candy and flowers he sends your way! Move on! Have nothing more to do with him! Remember when people tell you who they are,believe them!

Keep referring back to you list for your ideal Man. If you keep compromising, you will never reach your goal. Come on! Haven't you compromised far too much in your life up to this point? Your worth the time it takes. We invest time in looking good in our clothing and in our make-up. We invest time in our jobs and in our education. So take the time and do the work. For yourselves and for your future! Remember, your the only one who can change your future. You have the power! You have the pen needed to write a better story for yourselves. Take the time. Do the work. Recognize that you get out of any situation, just what you put into it. Know when things are not right for you! Cut your loses and move on. There are plenty good and wonderful Men out there who do right by the women they consider theirs. Some of you Ladies are so busy running after Mr. Wrong and his antics, that you would no recognize Mr. Right if he hunted you down, hit you over the head with a club,dragged you into his cave and said " Do you see me now"! As you audition or date, you are trying the situation on for size. To see if it fits! And I don't mean sexually! We'll get to that later. If the dress or the shoes don't fit, you don't keep them. You don't buy them. The same with the auditioner. Sometimes you know early in the dating process that, this will not work.(The dress does not fit right or doesn't look good on you). Don't waste your time or his.

Move on. There are other candidates. As said before, the dating or auditioning period is a time to evaluate the person that may be the special Man in your life. Making sure that you keep comparing him to your list! If the candidate does not meet your requirement, tell him thank you but your not the one. And go your separate ways. When a candidate does meet your requirements, spend some time investigating him. Give him some time and test the waters. If no red flags or strikes appear, continue on. This weeding out process should take about three to four months. It should not take longer than that to see if a candidate fits your requirements. If not. As I said before, move on. You spent enough time kissing frogs.

Now a word or two about sex. I'm all for it! I say do it as often and as frequently as you can but(you knew there was a but) only in a committed relationship. Never, never during the auditioning period! Why? There are two major reasons.

Men are able to distinguish between love and sex. They can put sex in a compartment and keep it there!

Women equate sex with love and have difficulty separating the the two.

Sex binds Women to Men, but not necessarily the other way around. This is one of the biggest mistakes Women make. And is one of the major reasons we get our hearts broken.

Women involve their hearts when they involve their bodies!

Men can involve their bodies and have no emotional attachment what so ever! Meaning that they can have sex with you and not care about you! Some are just a penis with a body attached looking for some vagina to implant itself into! Simple as that!

Women tend to complicate things. We may think that through

sex we are binding him to us when he sees it as a boody call! I know so many Sista's who think that what they have between their legs can and will keep that Man when they later realize that most Women have the same equipment.

If you are in need of sexual release, I advise you to get the battery operated or plug in kind! It won't break your heart and when your done with it, you clean it and put it in your drawer! A secret drawer!

Keep sex out of it as long as possible. It is very hard for a Women to pull herself out of even a dysfunctional relationship when sex is involved.

Your a very special special person now and you don't give what is special to the undeserving. Remember don't cast your perils before swine. Don't give the precious gift of yourself and your body to someone who doesn't respect and value you as the beautiful gift you really are. Nothing is special when anybody can have it! Right now, don't add this complication to your life.

As you are in the dating phase,remember you are the one who teaches other how you wish to be treated. Don't be afraid to let the auditioner know when you are displeased and when you feel you have been disrespected. Let the auditioner know that if this behavior does not stop, then be gone! You don't need a Man in your life to be fulfilled and you sure don't need anyone in your life who treats you badly. You are the foundation of any relationship you are involved in. This foundation must be strong or it will cave in. Stand strong!

Navigating the Waters

There are a few categories of Men who need to be avoided at all cost. You can take the detour if you want and end up road kill and scarred, or you can lean from the mistakes of other who have fallen for this type.

The first category of Men we will talk about, I will call Projects!

Projects are defined as Work! So much work! And whats worse, is the fact that the work may not even pay off! Many women end up spending so much money,effort and time! Some women think of the men as diamonds in the ruff. The problem is that no matter how much you keep polishing the damn thing, it won't get shiny! One such example is the Lady's Man! His major goal in life is to see just how many women he can stick his penis into.

He often looks good. Real good! Wares the right clothes, and looks good in them too! He will say or do anything to achieve their goal! And some will tell you who they are at the beginning. Most of you can recognize his type a mile away! You've even heard of his reputation. And did not listen to the warnings! But he looks good and says all the right things. And besides, he hasn't had your stuff yet!As you get in deeper the next thing you know, you see the back side of that very excellent butt as he walks out of your life on the the next conquest. Leaving you as road kill!

What baffles me is that smart, intelligent women who know in their hearts what type this Man is, (you may even have seen him in action) will still fall into the same damn trap. We rationalize the situation and think to ourselves that what we have between our legs will bind him to us! As I said before all women (who are anatomically correct) have the same equipment between their legs. And sex will not hold a Man who does not want to be there with you!

Another thing that baffles me is: Why would you want to be one of his many, instead when what you really want is to be someones one and only? Think very carefully before you involve yourselves in relationships with Men with multiple children. Especially if there are children from more than one women. Not to mention the baby,Mama drama that tend to follow this type. Be very wary of any Man who is not supporting his children from previous relationships! If he is not supporting the prodigy of his loins from other relationships,why would he support any offspring you may produce? Involving yourself with the Casanova's of the world,especially those who have multi pal children from multi pal relationships brings nothing but confusion and drama to your lives. Not to mention if you do end up marring one of these serial sperm donors, you are also responsible financially for his other children. Meaning that when he pays child support (and he should be paying it) your salary is factored in with his for the payments. Save yourselves the time,money and heat ache. When you see him coming, run in the opposite direction!

Mama's Boys

Mama's boys still have the umbilical cord attached to their Mother's. If you unwisely involve yourselves with him, you will find that there are three people in your relationship. Him, you and his Mother! You will also find that it is easy to replace a girlfriend but Mama is forever! Mama ain't going no where until death. And with some Men her influence will last long after death. And unless Mama relinquished the #1 spot, you won't ever be #1 with him! If a Man won't stand with you against his Mother, he won't stand with you when other obstetrical come along in life. I don't know about you but I prefer a Man with a back bone! One who is willing to stand when necessary even when it's against me if needed!

Married Men

I should not even have too address this issue. To me it should be a common scenes! If the Man is married, he is not yours! And 99.999% of the time, he will never be yours! Ladies, don't believe half of what he says! Sure he's smooth and says all the right things. He should by now! He has had enough practice! On his Wife! (Who he is also lying too). Why would you believe a Man you know is betraying someone else to be with you? Why do you think that he would loyal to you when he is betraying the women he has pledged his love and life too! He will string you along with smooth words,promises and lies. You will be alone on holidays because he will be spending those with the Wife and kids. The time you have with him will never be enough and only when he can steal the time away from his Family. But you will be the loyal one. Hoping and praying for the crumbs that fall from his table. Then one day you look up and find that months or even years later and you are no closer to your goal of having him to yourself! If you take this detour, you will end up where you started ,only bitter and feeling stupid. If your on this train, it's time to get off! And don't forget this fact. If you did reel this fish in, how would you be able to trust him,knowing he betrayed another women to be with you?

Predators In Church

I almost hate to bring this one up. There are some Men, who when they want a good Women, will go shopping for her in church! Yes Ladies! Just because you met the Man in church or the Man goes to church means he knows Jesus. Be just as cautious and continue the 3 strikes rule no matter the male source pool. These Men are trolling for the preverbal good girls. Someone they can influence, mold and control. Be careful when dating from a church pool. You may tend to let your guard down and take for granted that his ideals are higher. Hold all Men regardless of their sources to your new high standards. I know of a situation in which a Christian lady(a nurse) who got involved with a married Doctor. He knew he could not get to her in the usual way. He used the fact that she was a Christian and they began praying together. He convinced her that she was meant to be his and the fact that he was married with kids was a minor complication. After about two years when she felt so guilty about having sex with a married Man she would never have. She finally came to her senses Bitter and mad at herself and God. She knew going into this situation that:

He was a married man

For her, premarital sex was wrong.

Nothing in her bible supported her actions

He was a married man with children.

She did not start out to have an affair with a married Man but that is sure what she ended up doing. It is possible to get as close to someone your in prayer with as you can sexually. Be careful what type of situations you get yourselves into. The bible also says that you can tell a tree by it's fruit. As you listen to what any Man says, pay close attention to what he does. Make sure that the talk matches the walk before you take the chance.

One more caution Ladies. If you have children(especially girls) be very careful whom you allow into your life and the lives of your children.

It is never good for any child to see a parade of Men in and out of their Mother's life. I'm not saying don't date. But until you are sure of this Man and his intentions for you, don't introduce him to your children. It's not fair for them to form attachment and then have that attachment pulled out of their lives. Can you imagine the negative effects it can have on a child who's Mother's have had multi pal sexual partners parading in and out of their lives? Not to mention the damage it can do to the Mother / Child relationship. Having a male child won't save you, How do you think your young man learns to treat women? By the example that his Mother has set with the Man or Men in life. If you allow Men to disrespect you, how can you then expect your own Son to respect you? Remember when you bring a Man into your life and your children's life, you also bring along the influence and the drama of that Man. You are first and foremost the guardians at the gate of your home and in the lives of your children. Be careful who you open your gait too!

Sista's it is time to take off the rose colored glasses and stop deluding yourselves. Your love will not change any Man..Especially a Man who does not want to change! Leave the spineless men the Mama's boys,sperm donors and other projects to the less informed women and less knowledgeable women. Your time is too valuable to be wasted in such a way. If you are currently involved in a relationship with one of the previously described men, get out and get out now! You have wasted enough of you time and efforts on projects that bare no fruit! Don't waste one minute more!

You may have been in this relationship for some time and feel that you will be giving up. You can't give up on something that is going nowhere! If is has been a year, don't make it a year and one day! Stop taking yourselves for granted and letting others take you for granted also!

These types of relationships suck the life right out of you! They suck out your essence until until your nothing but a prune with all your vital juices gone! Remember, you no longer cast your pearls before swine! Let it go and save yourselves! Your better than this! And meant for better things. But until you let go of all the baggage your currently caring, you won't be free to fly to what is meant for you. Free yourselves! Save yourselves! Let it go!

Love

Some of us have no idea of what it is meant to love or be loved. We get our definition of love from soap operas,movies and other poor examples set for us. We have an idea of what it is,we even think it has to be painful and full of drama. But the best definition of love I've ever read came from the Bible. Makes sense when you think of it. Doesn't it! Do yourselves a favor and read First Corinthians chapter 13. Love is not the big drama that some of you are familiar with. It doesn't mean pain and should not hurt. Some of you are so hooked on the drama, that you think it as a requirement. The real deal is not filled with hills and valley's that constantly need to be scaled. It more of a constant security, a straight line,a safe place to fall with hands that pick you up if you do. A support system that stand you up or stands behind you when needed. If you don't want your Mama's drama, don't do what your Mama did! Wean yourselves off the drama and learn to appreciate the real deal. Learn to love the quite security that love offers. Learn what real love means.

What Does Change Bring

When you change the way you expect to be treated by others and the way you see yourselves, you also change the way you allow others to treat you .

Some of you may even lose some so called friends. Because you hold yourselves to a higher standard, you not only require more from yourselves but also from your friendships. There is always a ripple effect when change happens. When you change for the better don't expect everyone to be pleased! Misery loves companions and often gets upset when it loses one!

Some of your so called friends may try and drag you back to the place you once were because they are more comfortable with the old you. They would prefer for you to stay in that old comfort zone. The place you have just freed yourselves from! When they see you now taking responsibility for your life and your actions, they can no longer blame their actions on outside forces. They may be inspired by the new you or they may be fearful of the new you. If they take your example, that means that they now may have to make changes in their own lives. You may find that some of the people you have been calling friends are not! There are people who smile in your face but would rather you fail than succeed! Some even will try and keep you from unfolding. From expanding from changing. Sometimes to maintain the positive changes in you lives, you may have to change your friendships and even your environment ! You no longer think the same way they do and because your thought process is different, so are your actions. You are evolving into the person you have always wanted to be. Strong, confident in yourselves and in your abilities. With back bone enough to stand for yourselves and your opinions. You are now becoming a highly prized person not only to yourselves but also to others.

And the really good thing about this is that you also start attracting that same type of person toward yourselves. Thats right! You start attracting Men who are whole, strong and confident in their Manhood. Men who now see you as you see yourselves and or not intimidated with who and what you now represent.

Take Time to Think

Take some time between relationships to recuperate and to recharge. You should also take time and critique and spend some time in retrospection. If there are any lessons to be learned from a failed relationship, learn them now! Or you will repeat them later! Don't rush to put yourselves in yet another relationship. Spend some positive time with you. Shed all the baggage from the old relationship. Build yourselves up. Take yourselves to places you have always wanted to go. Treat yourselves to massages, facials and spend time with your girlfriends. Remember time spent with yourselves is never wasted. Also remember if you don't enjoy your own company, how do you expect others to enjoy it. Take classes in subjects your curious about. Always continue to learn! (It's good for the inside of you). Allow time for healing and sorrow when needed. You won't get to your goal if you don't endure some obstetrical along the way. Some of us try to avoid the pain and sorrow of situations that occur in our lives. The problem with that is, you really can't! You may think you can by activity or poring yourselves into others. But that only delays the inevitable. The quickest way to any destination is always a straight line. To get to it girlfriend, you have to go through it. Sometimes we suffer from the ill effects of a dysfunctional relationship. And we believe all the things told to us by that person we were in the relationship with. You need to listen to yourselves and not to the lies told you by someone trying to control you. If all you hear are the negative things told to you by him, you have a lot of work to do. Go back to the beginning! Fill in all those negatives with positives! Learn to see yourselves as you are and are progressing too! Not as he described you. Know that your voice and your opinion of yourselves is the only one that matters. Don't allow emotions especially destructive ones to keep you stuck in a place that tares you down instead of building you up! Growing pain are going to be experienced by anything that is expanding and unfolding as you are! If something doesn't grow or move, it stagnates.. Look up the word stagnate and see if you resembles the definition. Some of you have been beaten down so much mentally and spiritually that you don't know his lies from reality. Some have even been told that no one else will ever want you except the lier telling you that in the first place! If you don't deal with this problem now before seeking out other relationships, you may end up in the same nightmare over and over again. Because until you change the way in which you think and feel about yourselves, nothing else will change either! It all starts and ends with You! Never forget that fact!

Do the work that is necessary! Don't try and skip steps! Don't short change yourselves! You deserve the best that life has to offer. If you don't believe that, you won't get it. If you do believe that you deserve the best then you will get the best. Simple as that! It really is. We bring into our lives what we think we deserve! Take the time,do the work! You deserve what God has intended his children too have. The very best!

During this time of self retrospection, be happy. Be happy with the person you are and the person you are unfolding into. Fill yourselves with love and joy to overflowing. Remember, you are the party going someplace to happen. Let your light shine. Girlfriends,clean off the rust and clear off the dust if you have too. Put a battery into the light if you have too but turn the damn thing on! You will be surprised at what that light can illuminate and how it not only lights up your life but the lives of others. And you will also be surprised at who that life can direct into you life!

This book is really about the metamorphosis of you. About finding out who you really are and the value of your worth! About becoming the person you really are inside and knowing you are worthy. About not judging your worth or value by what others have told you. Learn to listen to your own voice.

If no one has told you how special, how wonderful, deserving,and worthy you are, start telling it to yourselves! Tell yourselves that you deserve all the God has intended for you to have and be on this earth! So, stop settling for the right now. We are in this for the long run and are willing to wait for the best. We invest in our educations and in our careers. Why not invest in yourselves. Your future, you peace of mind. This book is to let you know that you are whole,perfect and deserving just as you are. That being the best you that it is possible to be is the most wonderful gift you can give anyone!

God created us a perfect beings to enjoy this life given to us on this earth. He did not make junk! Don't let anyone convince you that you are less than your Heavenly Father has already told you that you are!

There is so many wonderful things to do here on the earth and to experience. So much joy to be had! Our lives are meant to be abundant. To have more than needed. But some of us spend our time in per suites that don't serve us. Like trying to turn a pigs ear into a silk purse! (Translation for those that need one) . Trying to turn an unworthy candidate into something he does not want to be. By being with Men who don't deserve you and never will. By putting yourselves in situations with Men you never should have been with in the first place! There is is Ladies! The plan,simple and honest truth that needed to be said! Accept the fact that you have made poor choices in the past. Then forgive yourselves! But most of all take responsibility for your mistakes and then LEARN FROM THEM! Do not! I repeat, do not continue to make the same mistakes over and over again! Save Yourselves!Take responsibility! Take time off with you! Go through the journey and learn to love yourselves! Truly love yourselves!

When you change the way you think,, you began to change your circumstances. When you change your circumstances, you change your life!

You deserve the best that life has to offer and it is still waiting for you to discover it! Instead of kissing a lot of frogs to see if they will turn into a prince. Start with kissing Princes instead! This also means stop being superficial and look deeper. Deeper than a pretty face, a fancy car and a pocket full of money! Your Prince may not drive the latest car or ware the hottest clothes. In fact your Prince may not be making the kind of money you would wish for him to be making. But he may know the value of the jewel of a women God has gifted him with. And know how to treat you like the Princess you truly are! Look at the heart of the Man! At his essence, at his soul. Your Prince may be no where near as handsome as you would like. But can gift you with his heart and his love. Which is really what you have been looking for! So look deep girlfriends. Look very deep!

I have more words of wisdom but we're going to change the format slightly to continue our learning process. So the rest will have to wait for another edition and another time. Remember Sista's, never let anyone steal your joy or put out your light. Never sacrifice yourselves to be in a relationship! Because if it is truly a relationship, you would not have to sacrifice you to be in it! You are whole with or without a Man in your life! Your relationship should never be about control of one over the other! But of cooperation, respect and compromise of both parties! For the good of both Your Man should be the one place and person where your loved and accepted for just being you! If you have yet to believe your value go back to the beginning and start again. Please! If you are convinced of your worthiness, your wholeness and of your perfection now and not at some future point, then your ready! You are ready to start a new and exciting chapter in your life. And on each page will be a great adventure with you unfolding into greater possibilities!!!! Go forth and seek out your future. And make it what is was truly meant to be. GREAT!!

Life Lession

As I had previously said in the beginning , it was my Husband's idea to write this book because of all the advice I have ended up giving to girlfriends. Maybe by sharing some of their stories, you too will be able to learn from their mistakes. Their mistakes may also keep you from following into their foot steps! Put yourselves in the situations these Sista's found themselves in and see just what your advice would be.

Princesses K. I met her about 14 years ago when she came to work on our unit. A beautiful,educated,smart and stylish black women. We became friends and began going to the gym together to work out. There were several men there who were interested in her. One on particular caught her eye. She was 6 years older than he and she worried about dating a younger man. I told her that Men have been dating and marring younger women since the beginning of time. Why not the other way around? Just to let you know the man did look good. From his very broad shoulders to his nice tight butt! (I am happily married but I'm not dead or blind). She finally accepted a coffee date with him to talk and get to know each other. He told her on their very first date that he was not looking for a serious relationship but just wanted to have some fun! Now I knew that my friend the Princesses was really looking for Husband material, so when she told me about the conversation, I said he is not for you. She was a little irritated with me because I first encouraged her to go out with him and now I say, he's not for you! I pointed out that the man just told you all he wants is some fun! Translation! Sex and only sex! I told her, if she was the type of a women who could have sex with a man and not get involved emotionally then it would be safe. But I pointed out to her, that she was not that type of women! She did not listen to me and reasoned that if he had hers then he would fall for her and feel for her. Translation! Trap him with her sex. Well instead of him falling for her, she fell hard for him. The Man would start showing up late at night at odd times! And even asked for money to jump start a new business venture. Well you can imagine how popular I was when I told her first not to give any money to a man who was using her for a boody call! I told her she deserved more than that! Some people are stubborn and have to learn the hard way. $1200 later and after she was declared road kill, she came to her senses. She was even angry with me because I said it was alright to date him. I pointed out that I also advised her not to have sex with him or give him money! She patched her heart back together and went on with her life. We are still good friends today! More on her adventures later!

The lessons that can be learned from her adventure! As stated much earlier in the book; When people tell you who they are. Believe them!

The man said on their first date that he was only in it for the fun! Much simpler and easier to take him at his word than th try and change him,his mind or his heart..

Traps are dangerous! And they tend to back fire as it did in the case of Princes K. Her plan to trap him with sex, trapped her instead! People who set traps for others are always in danger of falling into the traps they set!

Sex binds women to men and not necessarily Men to women!

Sista's, if the Man is a player, let him play somewhere else and with someone else's heart! Don't put yourselves in a position to be used and abused. You can't change someone who does not want to change ! And you cannot change a pigs ear into silk purse. Remember, don't cast your pearls before swine! Save yourselves! Stop trying!

Lady A:The first time I met this well dressed, beautiful full figures black women was when I floated to her unit. I'm a nurse and when we go to a unit that we don't normally work,it's called floating. We were in the back office of the nursing station. I was waiting for a fax and over heard her talking on the phone. She was speaking with a friend about her current Man. Saying that she had spoken with the man's ex-wife about him. The ex-wife had told her why she had divorced him. Saying that the only thing the Man told the truth about was his name. She had said that he would try to have sex with almost anything in a skirt and that she could have him and all his drama. I turned to her and said "I know you don't know me but , I could not help but over hear". "Run,!" "Run,long,fast and hard but get the hell away from him". Then my fax came and I left. About 6 months later we met through a mutual friend and became friends ourselves. She was a divorced Mother of a teenage son and very high maintenance. Loves to eat at the best places and brand name everything! As this time she was involved in a long distance relationship with a Man from Texas who was planning to relocate with her and her son in California. She had been to my home on several occasions and had met the kids and my Husband. She wanted her new Man to met my Husband so he would know at least one other Man in this state. So, they came over for drinks or we would go out and socialize at times together. My Husband and I were a little shocked when we first met this Man. He was such a simple kind of guy..Who's hobbies were working out and watching television. His favorite outfit of choice was jeans and T-shirt. Lady A the original high maintenance girl. The sophisticated, socialite prissy lady and the simple man struck me as an odd couple. When I asked my Husband what he thought of Mr. M., he said"There isn't much there". Trying to have a conversation with him was like pulling teeth". And my Husband gets along with everybody. As time passed she began noticing the relationship my Husband and I have and started to confide in me about her troubles with this new Man. Her plan was to marry this Man within the year, but he kept dragging his feet about setting a date. She and he had premarital counseling and the Pastor that was to marry them changed his mind. The Pastor even told Lady A. not to go ahead with the wedding. As she told me some of the troubles they had, I also questioned her wisdom in planning to marry this Man. They had different tastes and styles with everything. They had different sexual appetites. She wanting sex, more than he! She found out about some some calls he was making to an ex-girlfriend. And about flowers he had sent her. She had told our mutual friend that she would seek sexual satisfaction outside her marriage if he could not keep up. I said to her that I see several red flags and told her that she would be wise in stepping back and re-evaluating the idea of marring this Man. For some reason she was bound and determined to see this marriage through. Probably because she had purchased the dress and the shoes! I had to back off of pointing out the flaws in her wedding plans because she was becoming irritated with me telling her things she did not want to hear. I did not understand then or now why this girlfriend could not see what was right there in front of her eyes. This intelligent,beautiful, seemingly all together women was so wrapped up and strung out about a situation and was not facing the fact that were in her face. But I hoped the best for her. But the best did not happen. Things soon got worse. She found out the he had met someone else. A women she felt was inferior to her. A much planer, simpler less stylish and less complicated women. That really sent my girlfriend over the edge! Instead of just getting the lying, two timing man out of her life. She went to the other women and tried to ruin their relationship. She also tried to get him fired from his job. Things came to a head when he tried to attack her at work when she continued calling his boss and the other women. They have restraining orders against each other.

I never really thought that she was head over heels in love with this Man. I believe it was more the idea of marriage that she wanted more than the Man. I was so surprised at the way she acted and the venom she used when going after the other women. And in the effort to hurt him. She never succeeded in breaking them up. In fact he ended up marring the other women and is very happy with her. It took my friend about 8 months to a year to get over the situation. I'm not sure of the effect it had on her son.

The clues she missed or refused to see!

He kept dragging his feet about setting a date and really showed no enthusiasm when it came to the subject of marriage to her.

He kept contact with his old girlfriend without her knowledge.

They had very different interest and did not enjoy the same things!

They had very different sexual appetites, and he was uninterested in counseling to resolve the problem.

Her own Pastor refused to preform the wedding ceremony!!

He was lying to her about so many things. Lies which she caught him in.

She started to push her friends advice and her friends away because she did not want to see what was right there in her pretty face.

I believe the idea of marriage was so strong for my girlfriend, that she chose to ignore any other concept. I also believe that had she married that Man, she soon would have been divorced a second time. She could have saved herself much time, money, trouble and heartache if she had chosen to see what was actually there as it was. And not as she wished it to be. Ladies, open your eyes! See things as they truly are! See what is really there! Deluding yourselves and seeing the world through those rose colored glasses never, repeat, never serves you well!!! Get a grip! Your worth the real deal! Not some manufactured dream or fantasy. When Mr. Right finally gets your attention, thats when your reality can turn into the dream you always wanted. Only better! Because then it will be real!

My advice to my girlfriend was to take a vacation from all the time and attention she devoted to this man. And to attempting to destroy his new life and apply it to herself and her son(who was also hurting). I told her she needed to take time and explore the reasons she chose not to see the truth of the situation. There was something inside her that allowed her to over look the lies,deceit and all the strikes or red flags! Why was it that she could or would not see what was there in plain sight ? I told her that she needed to take time off and understand why she would do such a thing to herself and her son! Why was it that she was hell bound on marring a man who did not truly love her or treasure her? When she knew deep in her heart that he would not make her happy. She was living with him and not happy with him. What would have changed with a marriage license? Do you think she listened to me? More on Lady A. later.

Miss E... I first met Miss E. when she came to work on our unit at the hospital. My Husband still doesn't quite understand why it is we became friends because we are so different. She told me that she did not like me at all when we first met and that she thought I was in her words boogie and an Oreo. For those who don't know what an Oreo is, it's like the cookie. Black on the outside and white on the inside. My girl was from the hood and thought that because I chose to speak proper English instead of Ebonics that I was trying to be something that I am not. I pointed out that it was the use of English that got me my Carree and not Ebonics. I told her also that I was born black and since the stuff dose not wash off that I will die black also. And it was alright for her not to like me because I was busy loving myself and did not give a rats ass about her opinion. After awhile she started conversing more and more with me and told me of some of her problems. She was the mother of a 10 year old boy at this time and still hooked on the boy's father.(Whom I chose to refer too as a waste of skin) The man(it's hard for me to refer to him as such because he such a child) hasn't had a job since I have known her and I don't think he can even spell the word. He had played so many head games with her and constantly told her that she would not be able to get any Man better than him. He would be around on payday and be scarce the rest of the time. He never supported her in anything she wanted to do that may have advanced her. And never supported their son financially or emotionally! When she asked me for my advice, I told her that no one would be able to help her until she was willing to help herself. No man was able to use you as a rug to wipe his feet on, unless you lay down for him to do so! Until she thought better of herself, no one else would either. She seemed to have this cocky attitude at work with the other women but had an inferiority complex when it came to the so called man in her life. I told her if she believed the lies he told her about herself and did not consider herself worthy or special, all she'd get is more of the same. It took her awhile to find her value and see herself as worth the effort and kick him to the curb. The Man she is with today treats her and her son very well. And the baby's daddy,still does not have a job!

The lesson learned here is that there are Men who will tare you down just to make themselves feel good. Its a way of controlling and keeping you just where they want you. Which is usually under their feet. When a man is telling you that he is the only one who will ever feel anything for you! Know one thing! He is lying! If someone put you down constantly,it's for the reason of controlling you. This type of person will step all over and on you just to make themselves feel superior. Remember I said before, if no one has told you what you need to hear. That you are worthy,special and are a gift for the right Man. The only problem is, you are currently with the wrong one. Nothing will change until you do. So change and change now!

More on Princes K. She was working in Northern California at a small hospital and met a married M.D..They got to know each other and would take hikes and do the hot tube at their shared apartments. He was living at the apartment until the home he was building was finished. They talked and became very close but no hanky panky. She felt that since the Doctor and his wife did not share a normal marriage then they were not really married. Let me also state here that the Doctor was white and my friend is still black. I would not mention that if it were not for the fact that:

It was an small town in Northern California and 95% white.

The hospital was also small and 95% white.

Those that observed their behavior were not pleased.

The man was married!!!!!!!

Well she caused a lot of trouble for the wife who I'm sure had her reasons for living in Southern California. But apparently they had one if those marriages in which there is an arrangement. Princes K. had dreams of him leaving his wife and children and coming to her. After all she spent a lot of good money on Psychics who told her that he would eventually leave his life and share hers.

We had plenty conversations on this situation over a 3 year period. She caused so much confusion that she ended up losing the job at the hospital where they both worked. She finally came to the conclusion that this man and his wife had a kind of sick thing going on. He slept around with certain restrictions and so did she. My friend and he would have the most amazing conversations in which he would tell her who his current sexual partners were and what they did. She knew he had avoided having sex with her because she is one of those ladies with home and hearth on her mind. She is the marring kind and he was already a married man with no real intentions of ever changing anything. My girlfriend finally untangled herself from that situation and is now forever sworn off married men! After this experience she put herself back together and even rededicated her self back to God.

Ladies, married men are smooth and practiced. They know the right things to say and do to a women because they practice frequently. On their wives!

Don't believe that the man will leave his children and his wife for you! In probably over 95% of the cases the man never leaves! In the other 5% or so they may indeed leave their families and marry the other women. I have a question? How the hell are you going to trust a man who two timed his wife with you? And how do you have faith that if you produce children with this Man, he won't leave you and your family for another women? Remember the law of reciprocity which basically states what goes around,comes back around! If you involve yourselves in such, it will come back around to you.

More on Lady A: Unfortunately she did not listen to anything I said at the time and has had a succession of failed relationships. Some of very short duration but the latest did last about two years. The sad part is that it just ended and she's a little heart broken. She is a much stronger person now but I don't know if she has dealt with some of her old issues. Let me tell you about the latest Man. I think it was a powerful physical attraction that brought them together at first. But eventually they came up for air and began to talk. Will call him E. E is from Africa and had a much different idea about how marriage,family and relationships should go. Some of the differences were kind of comical and others steeped in tradition and very deep rooted. Most of these ideas would have had a lot of us running for the hills! But my girlfriend chose to stick it out.. Lady A. was still carrying some baggage from the earlier relationship I told you about when she planned to Marry the man she was living with at the time. One of the things that he said to her is that if he got married he would marry a female of his Mother's choice. He planned on having 5 children of more and he planned to send the oldest children to Africa to stay with his Mother. His Mother was in the process of choosing one of his cousins for him to marry. The plan was to bring the girl to America and get her a job. Then both were to work and send money to Africa to help support Mom and Papa. My girlfriend had a Son and had no plans of having other children. They also had some sexual differences but they seemed to be working that part out. His parents had disapproved of his relationship with my girlfriend because she had a previous marriage and she had a son from that marriage. In their culture,it was fine if the Man had been previously married with children but not the women. My friend had no serious plans with this man at first! So some of the differences did not bother her much. She was having fun with him and teaching him some things about American Women he was not aware of. Although this Man held licenses on two different medical fields he was always quitting one job and doing what I call job hopping. In the interim my friend helped him out financially. I was very annoyed with her when I found out she was giving him money. Mainly because he had the ability to earn much more than her in his chosen field of practice. All he had to do was go to work! And here it was that my friend not only had herself to support but her son also! She spoke to me about his family situation. Concerned about the plans his Mother had for him to marry a cousin. I told her at the time that if the Man won't stand up against his Mother for you than he won't stand for you in any situation ! I was concerned but she is a grown women and has to make her own way. She spoke to me almost crying a little later when she answered his cell phone and spoke to another women he had been seeing. And found out that some of the money she had given him, was spent on the other women! The other lady and my girlfriend decided too run a sting operation. So when he called the other lady, they had hooked it up to where my friend over heard the entire conversation and some of the very mean things he said about her. Near the end of the conversation, my friend spoke up letting him know that she heard the entire conversation. The other girl told him to get lost and never contact her again! My friend told him the same! She called me and told me all about it! But guess what? They were back together in less than two weeks. She said he put on the full court press and she forgave him! My mouth dropped open! Then I remembered to pick my bottom lip off the ground and started to speak my mind but my Husband squeezed my hand tight! Warning me that I was getting ready to put my foot in my open mouth! All I could do at the time was shake my head wondering just how much crap this women would take from this Man! I was about to find out! After a visit to his homeland(which she helped him financially to go to) he returned with bad news. He had been pressured by his Mother and was going to end their relationship to do his Mother's bidding. She came to me nearly in tears, telling me how much pressure was being placed on him. How much she loved him and would miss him. I just listened and offered comfort. With in two weeks they were back together. He had contracted malaria while he was in Africa and she nursed him back to health!

Thing went smoothly for awhile. She purchased a Condominium for her son and herself and life continued. E had discussed quiting work and going back to school to get a law degree. He even suggested that she marry him and support him while he went back to school! I was so afraid that she would do it! But she realized the flaws in that plan. She told him that she was already supporting her son and would not support a Man who could make twice her salary! I was so proud of her for not letting him use her in that way. As some time went on she started gathering some inner strength and maybe doing some inner searching. She continued her schooling and is working on her degree in public health. He was receiving letters and phone calls from Africa and family was continuing to pressure him about marring a cousin. He asked my girlfriend if it was alright with her if they continue the love affair when he married the other women? My girlfriend was devastated . After all they had been through This Man would still marry another, after expressing undying love for her. He said that he could not go against his Mother's wishes. He said that he did love her but his Mother did not care about his love for her. And to please his Mother and now dying Father, he would marry the girl they chose for him. My girlfriend had the balls to say not only no but Hell No! She had finally had enough! Which in my opinion took her about two years too long!

The lessons to be learned in this tale are:

When people tell you who they are, believe them. He admitted early in the relationship that he was a Mama's boy. We discussed that earlier in the book on the subject of Projects!

In a relationship with a Mama"s boy, Mama always wins. And always comes first. Sometimes even after her death.

He was two timing her with another women ! Even after they pulled the sting on the Man, she went back to him. If he cheats and lies to you, he is not for you!!!!!!

Men with no back bone cannot and will not stand with you or for you in the event of trouble.

And again I say, if he won't stand against his Mama for you, her won't stand for you in any situation!

Pastor said on one occasion that if you marry a child of the devil, your gonna have trouble from your Father-in-law! You will find yourselves competing with his Mother for his attention. She is going to give you trouble the entire time your with him.

Also remember I pointed out don't date what you don't plan to end up with.

Sista's, get a Man with a back bone. Not one attached to the umbilical cord of his Mother. You should be the Queen of your castle and not his Mama! There can only be one women , one Queen in residence at one time! If Lady A had talked the Man in question into marriage, she would have been at odds with her Mother-in-law and competing with her for the love, attention and affection of her own husband. And would have had to face the disapproval of her in-laws. Always coming in second in her own home. She could have saved herself if she listened to me. But she was hoping I was wrong. At times I even hope I'm wrong.

I would not have wished for my friend to go through all of that heart ache and pain. But we all operate on free will! And sometimes you see the pot hole and try to warn your friends and family. You can only hope that they listen! The biggest problem for me with this situation is that my Sista keeps taking very similar paths. And making similar mistakes. I do believe that she is much wiser in her choices now. And will find the Man just made specifically for her! She is a loving beautiful women and deserves much more than she has had!

This is why I advise some of my friends too just chill. Take time to rest and re-evaluate things. Before you can make it right you need to know what went wrong and why. Restore you reserves. Fill in all the holes in your life. Love yourselves. Understand why it is you have a tendency to take the same path. If you keep making the same bad choices you will have the same bad outcome. To continue on that same path is nuts! If you find yourselves on the road to that same place,change directions. Recognize the mistake and get the heck back on the right path. You better check yourself before you wreak yourself! Make a different choice! Chose a different path!

More on Princes K. I mentioned before that she was beautiful and smart and that after her episode in Northern California ,She dedicated her life back to God. She came to know a Man who helped her find and purchase her current Condominium. After becoming friendly with this Man for a while, he told her of a church he went too that may also meet her needs. She began attending this fabulous church (where some of the Movie Stars go) and loving it. She and C.(we will refer to him as C) began praying over the phone and began getting closer. She told me a one point that God had reviled to her that C. was to be her future husband.. I asked her to tell me about him. After learning a few things about the Brother in question, I told her that he may be the one for her but not right now! I said to her that he was not ready yet and in no position financially. I kept seeing financial trouble all about him,and that God was doing some work in the brother. I said it's like the time God told Sarah and Abraham that she was going to have a baby. Since Sarah was almost 100 she laughed when the angle told her she would bare a child. (actually it is a very good story in the bible with a multitude of lessons which you all should read). There were years before the baby was born to Sarah. Although God had promised her this prize,she had to wait for it. That is what I was telling my friend. That although C. may be promised to her, she needed to wait until God finished the work in him. He was always promising to take her here and there but was working a lot of overtime trying to keep his business afloat. My friend became more enamored of the Man even though it seemed he never made time to see her and seemed to break a lot of promises. As time passed he began to struggle more with the Real Estate business. She felt bad for him and did not want to see him fail. I told her that what he was going through,God was putting him through. I told her that she would only slow down the process and possibly get herself into trouble financially if she got involved. I told her she would be stepping out of the hedge of protection God had her in and she would end up having to face the consequences. She said to me that she saw this

Man as already hers even though he did not return her feeling as the time. I did remind her that this promised man, was not her Husband yet and did not deserve to be treated as such! I said to her not to get financially involved! But,she loved him and did not want to see him fail. This Man saw himself as a guide and teacher to my friend and was not involved romantically. But because she was looking at the future and not at the present, she began helping him out financially. Oh it started out small. Paying the telephone and light bills at the home and office. The car repair bills. Helping get one of the houses he owned ready to rent. Lending him money for his new business venture. And finally securing a loan that will take her 6 years to pay off. A lot of this she did not tell me until she had already done it. When she told me that in total it was a little over $100,00.00 she had given this man, I was so appalled! I had to tell her I would call her back because I had to sit down and absorb this information. My Husband asked me what was going on and I told him .(He knows Princes K and likes her). He could not believe that Princes K fell for that! Especially since there was no sex involved! You know Men! My Husband thinks that C. is a con man working the churches. He may be right! As it stands C. has only payed back less than $1200.00 of the $100,000.00 that he owes my friend(who by the ways still loves this man). As things stand now she has finally reached the financial limit with this man. And now sees that he is and has been ungrateful for all of her sacrifice and treats her with indifference. Once this man had the nerve to tell her that she was selfish!!!!! She wanted to spend his birthday with him. You know maybe lunch after church and a walk and talk on the beach! That was the least this money pit could have done as some form or repayment to my friend. But it wasn't to be. He called up the night before their date and wanted to change things. He could spare two hours with her and then spend the rest of the day with his friends. She was upset about the fact he would not give her the time after she had given him all that money. So she called him back and told him to spend the day with his friends because she deserved more than two hours. That is when he left a message on her phone stating that he thought that she was selfish at wanting his entire day! Not one of his friends had stepped up to help this man at all. In fact, I bet his friends don't know because Princes K had provided him with enough money that no one knew that he was in financial trouble.

As another of my long time friends is fond of saying " He ripped his drawers with me". Meaning he had really made me angry. There's more I could tell you but as things stand now she is in debt. But God has provided a way for her to put her life back together financially. She had told me that she thought she was meant to help C. because she had opportunity to work a lot of overtime at the hospital. I told her that helping out C was a desire of her heart! And that God was fulfilling the desires of her heart, not that she was meant to give all that money to a Man that was not hers! I believe that if God had not provided her a way to make a lot of money with overtime,she would have secured a loan for much more than she has done thus far! I told her that she had allowed this man to take advantage of her and she had done so, with the warnings I had given her. That she needed to take responsibility for her actions. After all the time she has known me (over 10 years now) I have never been wrong in what God has given me to tell her. And I told her at ever step, not to get involved financially because she would bring all the trouble he was in, to herself! She is lucky to only have to pay back $30.000.00. She could have been in a much deeper hole than she presently is. Lets look at some of the things that got our Sista in that hole.. So that hopefully you won't fall in to one also.

Women have a tendency to be fixers. We try to fix to a situation. We start seeing a situation as it will be under our influence and not as it is right now. We project our feeling into a situation thereby distorting the view. We see the future and not the present. If this is the situation in which you find yourselves in, step back and step back now. Take off the rose colored glasses because this never,never serves you! We believe our love will make all the difference! And it may! But only to the right Man. And if it is the right Man, you will not need the filter your using to see the situation as you wish it to be,but as it truly is! Why waste your time and effort on someone who is not appreciating it. If God indeed has this man for our dear sister, then he is powerful and skillful enough to do what he has promised you. When you try to hasten the process, when you try to manipulate the situation, you will only cause yourselves more problems. When dealing with the promises of God, we need to let God be God. By that I mean, don't get in God's way. We as a generation are not into delayed gratification. We are a microwave generation! We want what we want and we want it now! Sometimes when God makes us a promise,we start counting the minutes or looking at our clocks or watches. When many times we need to look at the calender instead! If you remember the story of Abraham and Sarah we referred to earlier, She had some difficulty accepting the promise God made to her. When she did not become with child in a timely manor,she arranged things herself`! She arranged for her Husband to have sex with her hand maiden((Hagar)who did become pregnant! That child was Ishmael! At God's appointed time, Sarah did indeed become with child as God promised. When Isaac was born, there was great jealously between the women! Eventually Hagar and Ishmael were exiled from the tribe! But God cared for the stranded mother and child after Hagar cried out to him to save her son. To this day, a battle still exist between Ishmael and Isaac. Israel and Palestine are still at war today! And it all started when Sarah got in the way of God's plan!

When Princes K got the message from God! She decided to take things in her own hands. Instead of waiting on the Lord, she took control! Even though she had been warned not to contribute financially,she did anyway! She even admitted later that God had told her that there would be a time of preparation before the promise would come to pass! But she got ahead of God and tried to hasten,hurry and make the promise happen in her time!!!! When ever we try and control or manipulate a situation, we stop God from doing his work. He created this universe with a thought and a word! Why is it that you think you can do better than he? I believe that the financial crisis in this Man's life was from God. I believe that God was using the crisis to do a work in this Man's life. When my friend gave him money to stop the professional and personal financial bleeding, she stepped into the mess the man had already made! She tried to change God's plan for this man,because she did not want to see him fail! Instead of seeing the situation as it was,she chose to see it through a filter. She told me once " This Man is mine, so I will get all this money back". My response to her was that this man was not her Husband, and should not be given the privileges of one." Until he was one! She worked a lot of overtime and made personal sacrifices to give this man money. When she depleted her savings account, she took out a loan and even gave him access to a credit card. This Man made all kinds of promises he did not keep. Yet my friend continued to ignore all the advice I had given her. Now since the Man owes her so much money with no ability(or intention) of paying it back. He no longer returns her phone calls. And as I already stated she is more than $30,000.00 dollars in debt because she tried to hurry God's plan. Because she did,she created her own Ishmael! And now has to deal with it. She has taken responsibility for what she has done and is now allowing God to be God! After all, he sure can't do any worse than she has done! She could blame the whole thing on the Man but in order to do so ,she have to admit ignoring the good advice of her friends! So she has to except her role in this problem. By getting in the way of God, she only delayed what was inevitable! Instead of making things happen faster, more work needs to be done and undone! Not only will God have to complete the work he was trying to accomplish in the brother's life, he also has to undo the hurt caused between the two parties!

The other thing our sister ignored is that,when people tell you who they are. Believe them! He said in the beginning, that he saw himself in only a teaching role. I'm not discounting what God told my Sista! What I am saying is that just because God told you something, does not mean he told the same to another. If the Man hasn't got the word yet,don't try and stuff it down his throat. The saying,let go and let God is so approbate here. Manipulation and intimidation is equal to witchcraft in the bible. Do not employ this in any of this in your dealings with people. Allow yourselves to be blessed by the one from whom all blessings flow. Don't try and make the situation what it is not. That strategy never,never serves you!

As I said before, my friend created her own Ishmael when she stepped out of the hedge of protection provided by God, and into this man's financial hell. She will be in debt for the next 6 years because of her big heart. Her saga continues! She now is content on sitting and waiting on the Lord. Learn from her situation! Please! When in doubt, lead with your head and not your heart. That way you wont get your heart trampled! I hope to have good news for you in the next installment of Sista Chat 2 about her situation.

Remember the warning about there being hunters in the Church! Some ,not so good Men, use the Church for their trolling ground. Be sure of the fruit that the tree produces! Just because you met the Man in church does not mean that he is not a devil in Christian clothing!

Maybe a couple more examples of life lessons before we end and give you time to absorb all of what is being said here:

Let's talk about Ms. F: I've know her all my life . She got married young. And from the outside looking in, all looked well. There are several things that I admire about Ms. F. She was the least favorite in her family, and it showed. Yet when her Mother and Father were incapacitated, she cared for them until their deaths. She also helped raise her sisters children, when her sister went to prison for a while. During this time she put herself through school and got her R.N.

She is the Mother of 3 sons and all are doing well. What I did not know is what was going on behind the seen.

I found out what was going on after the fact. My girl ended up in the hospital after an attempted suicide! She had what I call a high maintenance Man. One of those who is never where he says he is. And very unfaithful! She had caught him with several women. She had even gotten into the habit of getting in her car and riding around town looking for him when he did not come home. Her sister told me that at times when he came in late, she would make him drop his pants to inspect him! Yes ladies, she would inspect his genitals!

After years of this, he finally left her for another Women. That is when she shot herself! It was a tragic and desperate act. And the real pitiful thing is, that her lying in that hospital with a self inflicted gun shot wound and her Husband still left her!

She graduated from school and was now making a lot more money than she ever had before. It was a few years later that I ran into her again. I had heard that she had re-married and was doing well. As we were talking she let it slip that she was working 5 to 6 days a week. That got my attention! Mainly because we work 12 hour shifts in the hospital. Nursing is a very high stress job so when someone works more than 4 days, it's because they need the money! It's also dangerous to be too tired in nursing. You can make mistakes that can cause someone their lives! I pulled her aside and asked her what was going on? I knew she had inherited the house from her Mother so she had no mortgage payment. Why was she killing herself? So she told me. When she re-married, she decided to help her Husbands business out financially. She also purchased two new cars, a new boat and a work van for her Husband! But the kicker was that now she had found out while she was at work, this Man was driving another Women around in the car she was paying for. Her new Husband had emptied her bank accounts and moved out. She apparently got into it physically with the other Women and her Husband called the police on her! He also had written the State Bord attempting to have her license revoked!! I had trouble believing that after her first Husband, she would get herself into a situation with another high maintenance Man. I figured she was going through enough, so I just let her talk of her plans. She stated that she was going to get herself out of that situation and the marriage.

But guess what she did? She sold her home and moved to a new State! The problem with her new start, is that she took the same old Man with her! Why is it Women choice the same path and expect a different outcome? Now she still works about 5 to 6 (12 hour shifts) a week. Her Husband is disable and on renal dialysis 3 days a week. Ms. F. is having some trouble in her choice of State. She has apparently had difficulty at some of the hospitals she has worked in, and some will not allow her back as an employee. She has even borrowed money from my Mother, which she hasn't been able to pay back!

If you find yourselves in this type of negative spiral, get off the merry go round.

What can we learn from our Ms. F.?

Some of us are hooked on the drama. Why on God's green earth did she allow herself to be treated in such a way? Why did she stay in a relationship in which she knew, she could not trust her

Man? And the biggest of all. Why did she repeat the same situation with a different Man? We all have choices to make. Some choices free us and others bind us. Don't keep doing the same thing and think that something will change, Nothing changes until you do! It doesn't matter if you change State's or houses. If you take the same mess with you.

When people tell you who they are? We keep hearing that! This man not only used her, her cars and money to date other women. He tried to take away her lively hood! By writing letters to the State Board,he was attempting to have her license revoked! Yet she stayed married to him,sold her paid off home and moved across the country! What the hell does she expect to change, except the location in which he is disloyal to her. Especially since he no longer works and has plenty of time alone. This bright,educated,smart women got herself out of a hellish situation and than put herself right back in the pit she crawled out of! Ladies if this sounds like you, it is up to you not only to get yourselves out of that situation but keep yourselves out! Don't keep making the same mistakes over and over again. Learn from them! Learn the lessons that are meant to be taught. Until you do, your at risk to keep repeating them over and over again!

This last story I have for you was deliberately saved for last because it has such far reaching effect.

I met this flashy Southern Bell shortly before I married my Husband. At first glance Miss SB. Seemed to have everything. The big house, the Corvet, nice clothes and a seemingly well known Man. If I had not been a house guest on several occasions, I would not know much about the relationship of Miss SB. and her Man . The

Man in question was in one of those profession,which is considered illegal but brings in lots of money. He was a former armature boxer and well known in the town in which they lived Although Miss SB. Seemed to be living the high life, I began to notice what price she payed. She had a 10 year old son from a previous marriage. I found out much later that her Husband was a regular,nice guy. One who had a plan to work his way up the ladder and give his family a stable but unexciting life. She threw this man away for the excitement and the thrill of this new flashy,popular Cadillac driving, drug selling ,ex-boxer. She and her ex-husband had an arrangement in which their son went to his Father in the summer and stayed with SB and her drug selling, ex-boxer the rest of the time..

When I did visit there were some things I though of as strange, Although R.(lets call the boxer R.) stayed at home most of the day,SB. worked outside the home. But what I thought was strange, is that she had to give R. her entire paycheck! He would then decide how much she needed for house hold expenses. I also noticed that he would go out and party on the weekends, without her! The other thing I found strange is that she would iron his clothes in order for him to go out! Every now and then when my Husband and I would go out on the weekends,we would run into him with other women! It was very important for her to have the home,the car and even the Man! No matter how he treated her! All this, her Son observed year after year. My Husband and I went on vacation once with them. Something that has and will never happen again! We traveled by car from Little Rock Arkansas to Orlando Florida . They literally argued all the way! They got on my nerves so bad, I almost started smoking again! I wanted to just shoot myself in the head to have a little peace and quite. They argued over the most stupid thing. No matter what she said to him, he found fault with it. Listening to them I noticed that he gave her very little credit for anything. When things went wrong, he blamed her! When things went right, he took credit for it,even when she did all the work! I just could not believe this loud ,out spoken,opinionated Women, was taking all that crap from this Man. But when I listened to her conversation with others, she really liked bragging about what it was that she had! The big house,the nice car and clothes! She was willing to take all that from him in order to keep what she though was important! Well as stated before as a quote from Pastor. Sin will take you further than you want to go. Keep you longer than you want to stay. And cost you more than you want to pay! R. had been under surveillance by the police department for sometime. And was set up and busted! SB. Was also arrested and her Corvet impounded. Their money was seized. She was fired from her job and they lost the big house. R blamed her, and the stress of the situation finally broke them up for good! Unfortunately, thats not all! Remember the son? He lost all respect for his Mother. One day my Husband and I were visiting her in her roach infested apartment. And her Son came by. They began arguing and She went and got a baseball bat to intimidate him with. The next thing we knew,her Son had her pinned to the dinning room table with the bat she had been swinging around. He's just calling her every name in the book and we thought that he was going to hit her. My Husband had to literally pull him off her! It tore my Husband up! Here was this child that we remembered as a straight A student with such sweet manners. Now almost a grown Man nearly striking his Mother! We haven't seen him since! He followed in his so called Step Father's foot steps and began dealing drugs. Every time we have gone back to visit, he has been in jail. If he repeats one more time, he will be in for 20 years! I'm sure that when SB. got the hots for this so called exciting Man, she did not take into consideration the long term effect R. would have on her Son or on Her! Who taught her Son to disrespect her! Who taught her Son, that the shortcut was the only way to go! That school was not cool. But money made by selling drugs was! Who put not only her Son but herself in a position for the above to happen? She did when she took this man over her Husband! By the way, her ex-husband is now the one with the big house with a pool. He has the stylish car and money! The only thing is that he is sharing that house, pool and car with another Women and another Son!

What lessons can be learned from the experiences of our SB?

1. It is vital that you be careful whom you allow into your child's life. When you bring people into yours and your child's life, you also bring them and their drama. You are the only gate keeper there is for your child. There is no one else. Be careful who you let inside.

Some of us equate drama with excitement and lack of drama as boring. Dependable is not boring, but something that can be counted on.

When we allow ourself to be mistreated by men, and this treatment is witnessed by your children. We do them harm. We teach our girls that men are to mistreat them, and we teach our boy's that we are unworthy of being treated well. We let the Man that mistreats us, teach our Son's how to treat us and other women.

It teaches our Son's that we don't deserve better! And some of us are then mistreated by our own children! Because of who we have allowed in our lives! And how we have allowed the Men in our lives to treat us!

You play such an important role in the lives of your children's. Never take it for granted that what you do and how you do it, is not important! Not to mention who you do it with! Know your value. Know that what you think of yourselves will determine how you allow yourselves to be treated by others.

It starts and stops with you! You have all the power! Don't give your power away! Especially to any who don't appreciate it or deserve it!

What and How I Learned

Before my beginnings were the beginnings of My Parents. My Father was born in a place called Hooks Texas. He was what was referred too a dirt poor. He actually had to put paper in the soles of his shoes at times to cover the holes. His Mother,my Grandmother would be identified today as possibly schizophrenic and beat him just because. She would be angry at my Grandfather but beat my Father because he looked like the Man she was angry with. When he would try to study and do his homework, he would be admonished by her for using up too much oil. So if he did not get his homework done by dark,it did not get done. He met a Man he admired who was able to fix anything on a car and saw what he thought may be a way out of poverty. He joined the army, and when he was discharge took advantage of the schooling offered by the G.I. Bill. He was very careful not to bring any children into the world until he was in a position to give them the things he was never given as a child. He made promises to himself, that he intended to keep. On a collision course with my Mother, they met in college. My Mother, the oldest of 7,was attending Preview University to obtain her teaching degree. From what I understand, there was something instant between them. My Grandmother was unset with my Mother's decision to marry my Father because she had an opportunity to be in the same position as Mahilya Jackson! The famous gospel singer. My Mama can sing. But from what I got from Granny, she gave up a singing career to be my Father's wife!

My Mother had a very good influence on my Father. She helped him with self confidence and to stand up for himself and his beliefs. She stood beside him as he improved his skills and himself ,often with her prodding. Both my Parents helped to put the other through school. One thing both thought was important not only to them but for the entire Black race, was education. They knew that education meant the difference between being able to provide for the family and the life that most Black people were experiencing. Especially in the South, which is where they both were born. Both my parents experienced scorn from friends and family members alike telling them that they were trying to be something they were not. They were told ,why don't you just give up the schooling and enjoy life. Why spend all that time studying when no one will give you a good paying job anyway. I remember even as my brother and I were young. We would spend the summer in Texas while one or both Parents would go to summer school. I remember when my Mother got her bachelors degree and helped my Father get his masters degree both in education. I also remember about a year or two before this time,my Grandmother (my Mother's mother) got her masters degree in education.

I heard several conversations which my Aunts or Uncles on both sides were telling my Parents that they were sheltering us too much. That they were over protective.

There were things that my cousins were allowed to do and

places they were allowed to go that my Brother and I were not. I have memories of one Uncle in particular who I knew at an early age had something against my Parents and my brother and myself. He never had anything good to say to us as children but seemed to be the first to criticize. My Parents on the other hand were always encouraging us and telling us that there was nothing we could not do. They always emphasized how important is was to get an education and just assumed that we both would go to college. And we both did!

There we many experiences I received and many lessons that I learned from both my Parents. One is that in all things they loved and respected one another. It showed in the way my Father treated my Mother. He would not allow anyone even us children to speak to my Mother in any other than a respectful way. They always seemed to support each other in all their per suites to advance up the ladder and made many sacrifices for our welfare. They worked extra hours or jobs to make sure that we had all the things we needed and a lot of things we wanted. We both played musical instruments and I had the opportunity to play in a youth orchestra for two years. I was also given the opportunity to be a couple of plays at the University of Red lands when I was in Jr. High School. I did have some self -esteem issues, manly because I was the only black female at an almost all white school. My Mother had a way of turning things around and making it seem that I was the fortunate one because I had so many to chose among as friends. It's a good thing she had that quality because I needed it I was for some of the people I met the only Black person they knew. There were many times I saw that there was much love between my Parents. One such time was when my Grandmother on my Father's side came to stay with us for a summer. My Grandmother was a piece of work. As I told you she was very abusive to my Father and was just being a major pain in the back side the entire time she was there. My Mother tried to be accommodating but the more my Mom tried to please this Women,the worse she became. According to her, she was the one who put my Father through college by selling a cow. Not that it was the little sty pin he got from the GI bill and the fact that he had to work all kinds of odd jobs to continue school and eat. She did not like our religious affiliation or the way in which my Parents were raising us. My Mother was breaking out in hives because of her harassment. Not to mention the usual peace we felt in our home was no longer there. Well, my Father had enough after Mom started breaking out, and Dad asked his Mother to pack her bags. He told her that she had caused enough confusion in his home that he had welcomed her into. But it was now past the time that she left! I don't have to tell you how happy we were that she was on a plane that night heading back to Texas. There were several times in which I saw my Parents stand for each other against other Family Members. One incident in particular stands out in my memory. My Mother's Brothers (all but George) were what I referred earlier as projects. Man-boys is a good name for them,because they look like Men but act like irresponsible boy's. In several instances they were unemployed. At one time my Father not only taught High School but leased a gas station. Remember back in the days in which a real person would put gas in your tank? Well thats about all my Uncles had the education to do. They were part of the crowed that told my Parents that they were waisting their time going to school.

70

Funny how life works out isn't it? Well during this time, my Uncle was working at the gas station as an employee. We found out that he was embezzling funds When my Father asked him about the missing money, my Uncle became belligerent and began cursing my Father out. Instead of admitting wrong doing, my Uncle began lying about the incident and the next thing I know, there is this big Family pow wow. As I remember it, my Uncle was trying to get the Family on his side acting like the money was his to steal. He even acted as if it was my Mother's fault for talking my Father into helping him out by giving him the job in the first place. Everyone was yelling at my Father, when my Mother stood up and asked each and everyone of them a question! Where were you when we were in need? But do you remember who you called when you needed something? She pointed out several instances in which each and every one of them had come to her and my Father for money or favor! And in all instances had not returned the loan . She pointed out that there was nothing she could come to them for because none of them had anything she needed or wanted. Also that most of them would not have what they had, if it had not been for her and my Father. I did not know why at the time but I felt so proud of my Mother! She pointed out that each and every one of them had come to my Parents for financial assistance and that they had helped them. And here it was my Uncle was not only being helped by my Father ,but was stealing from not only my Father but from her and her children! All my up set ,ungrateful Uncles were than invited to leave the property and not come back until an apology was issued to my Parents. My Uncles were shocked at my Mother's stand and tried too hold a grudge but they needed money .And eventually had to come back and apologize. I always thought my Uncles had a lot of nerve. To steal from my Parents and then act as if it was their privilege to do so! And that it would be allowed or accepted by my Parents. Some people have a lot of nerve, don't they?

Once when I was about 13 years old I had a fight over the phone with my so called boyfriend at the time. I was crying and my Father asked me what was going on. When I was able to get it out he gave me a hug and told me to go wash my face. After I got myself together my Father sat me down and gave me what was his male/female relationship talk He told me that I should let no male bring me to tears. He told me how special I was and gave me some tips on handling the situation . Some of that information is still serving me today. How special I felt knowing that the one male figure in my life not only loved me and thought that I was special but gave me the confidence to handle other situations with men.

Even when my Parents disagreed, and there were plenty of those times! They never got into name calling! They never tried to force the others agreement. It was all about cooperation and compromise! They would always talk thing through! In the end they always ended up supporting each other.

I have been fortunate in the fact that I had what is termed as a functional family. A family in which my Mother was a strong women married to a loving strong Man . A Man who not only treated his Wife with love and respect but also his daughter. There is much to be learned when watching your Parents interactions! There are many instances in which my Parents showed me how to interact with someone I loved. I can understand that some of you women may have more difficulty with the concept especially if you were not privileged to have a Father or positive Male or female role model in your lives. As I suggested earlier, you may need to find a role model and observe their interactions.

In the early days of the Church is was the older women who taught the younger one's how to love their Husbands and care for their children's. Things are different these days and we have to learn a lot of things on our own. We don't have the guidance we need. That is part of the reason for this book. Even with the proper guidance we get lost. And for those who are lost, my hope is that a little of what has been said here offers some aide to you and will minister to your heart. To encourage you and build you up. To give you a foundation of confidence,strength and self respect. Anything built with that foundation will stand. As said before some of you do not have the example that was set for me. Some of you have no good male or female role model in your lives and have had to struggle through on your own. If possible, find a role model to observe, them and their interactions. Maybe even ask them advice. Use the example I have from my Parents! But know if you believe in yourselves, you can and will accomplish what it is you set out to do!

My Parents have been married for 53 almost 54 years (it will be 54 years in December) and are still a riot to watch. I feel so lucky to have had the Parents that I have. It takes a certain amount of retrospection, to know that you have been truly blessed in life. And I have been! To have had such a good examples of male/female influence in my life. And to still have my Parents with me. They are 73 and 79 respectively and still in good health. Although my

Mother was seriously ill earlier this year and scared me good. But, God has restored her and she is and I quote "As sassy as ever ".

I would like to leave you with this thought. You attitude determines your altitude. Meaning that when you believe, there is nothing you can't do! Nothing can stop you but you! Let go of all the negative thoughts that hold you back. Erase that tape that goes through your mind telling you that you will never be able to do this or do that. Place positive things on that tape and play it often! All the negative things in your life that don't serve you, let them go forever. When they knock on your door, don't let them back in. Tell yourself what you need to hear about you. That you are worthy. That you are deserving. And that here is nothing you cannot do or be if you want it badly enough! So go and be the best you that it is possible too be!

Notes

Notes

Notes

Notes

Notes

Notes

Notes

Notes

Notes

Notes

Notes

Notes

Notes

Notes

Notes

Notes

Notes

Notes

The Author's Page

The Author of Sista Chat currently makes her home in Southern California. Since this is her first book she still keeps her day job as a Registered Nurse. She currently lives with her Husband and two of her three Son's along with their pet rabbit Cadberry, and her beautiful pupy Missy.